AREA 51
ENDURING MYSTERIES

KEN KARST

Published by
CREATIVE EDUCATION

P.O. Box 227, Mankato, Minnesota 56002
Creative Education is an imprint of The Creative Company
www.thecreativecompany.us

Design and production by Danny Nanos of Gilbert & Nanos
Art direction by Rita Marshall
Printed in the United States of America

Photographs by Alamy (Andia, David Coleman, Pictorial Press Ltd), Shutterstock (anyunov, B747, Chromatika
Multimedia snc, Anthony Correia, Creativa, CristinaMuraca, Claudio Divizia, dvande, emattil, Everett Collection, Globe
Turner, Fer Gregory, Chris Harvey, justasc, Krasowit, MarkauMark, Phil McDonald, mikhail, mj007, Mwaits, n7atal7i,
Alexandru Nika, Photobank gallery, photoBeard, Steve Reed, schmaelterphoto, SSSCCC, Maria Starovoytova,
Alexey Stiop, Stocksnapper, Teia, vvoronov), SuperStock (Everett Collection, StockTrek/Purestock, Tips Images)
Series logo illustration by Anne Yvonne Gilbert

Library of Congress Cataloging-in-Publication Data

Karst, Ken.
Area 51 / Ken Karst.
p. cm. — (Enduring mysteries)
Includes bibliographical references and index.
Summary: An investigative approach to the curious phenomena and mysterious circumstances
surrounding Area 51, from conspiracy theories to claims of extraterrestrial sightings to hard facts.

ISBN 978-1-60818-399-9
1. Unidentified flying objects—Sightings and encounters—Nevada—Juvenile literature.
2. Area 51 (Nev.)—Juvenile literature. 3. Air bases—Nevada—Juvenile literature.
4. Research aircraft—United States—Juvenile literature. I. Title.

TL789.2.K47 2014

358.4'170979314—dc23   2013036073

CCSS: RI.5.1, 2, 3, 6, 8; RH.6-8.4, 5, 6, 7, 8

FIRST EDITION

9 8 7 6 5 4 3 2 1

CREATIVE EDUCATION

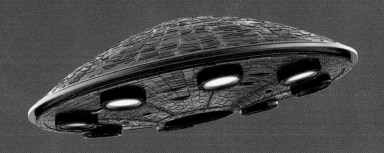

Table of Contents

Introduction   4

Can't Get There from Here   6
  A Good Guess   15
A Man-made Mystery   16
  The Cold War   25
Folks and Fiction   26
  Saucers: Keep Left   35
Straight Stories, Stranger Stories   36
  Roswell   45

Field Notes   46
Selected Bibliography   47
Websites   47
Index   48

When Bob Lazar told a television interviewer in 1989 that he'd been researching captured flying saucers at a base in the Nevada desert, trying to figure out what made them fly so fast, the name "Area 51" suddenly became the key code word for government **conspiracies**. Bright lights and fast-moving objects had been regular features in the night sky above the restricted military zone north of Las Vegas since the 1950s, causing many people to wonder what was going on out there. But those who worked there were forbidden to tell anyone, even their spouses, what they did or saw. The United States government, which controlled the land, refused to acknowledge the existence of any sort of base. Lazar believed such secrecy was standing in the way of greater scientific progress and broke his silence. Hearing stories from a scientist who claimed to have studied extraterrestrial technology confirmed many Americans' suspicions that beings from outer space had already visited Earth. People began to wonder about what the government was concealing and feared whatever beings could have been responsible for creating technology that seemed so advanced. Suddenly, Area 51 was on the map, in a big—but still invisible—way.

CAN'T GET THERE

FROM HERE

Area 51. It sounds like a railroad yard or a spot on a game board, not a legend like Shangri-La or Atlantis. But for more than half a century, Area 51 has been at the center of extraordinary American stories. Which of them are true? Which aren't?

One reason why Area 51 has spun up so many vivid tales, perhaps, has to do with the fact that nearly everything about it has been officially denied, or simply left unexplained. The *New York Times* once described it as "a base so secret it doesn't exist." And it's a well-known **irony** that secrecy often attracts the spotlight.

But Area 51 does exist and has played a key role in American **aeronautics**, politics, and defense, even though its **budget**, operations, and employees have rarely been made public—sometimes not even to the president. When Lyndon Johnson took office in 1963 upon president John F. Kennedy's death, he had never heard of Area 51 and had no

knowledge of a revolutionary spy plane that was being developed there. Area 51 has also been central to conspiracy theories and other scenarios involving military plots, government deception, cooperation with extraterrestrial beings, international intrigue, and fantastic technology.

It's easier to find Area 51 than it used to be, when even U.S. Geological Survey maps didn't label it. Google Maps can take you right there and even show you runways, hangars, and other buildings—views that not long ago could have gotten you shot down if you were a pilot, arrested if you were hiking close enough to see them, or praised if you were a foreign spy. Physically, Area 51 is located about 80 miles (129 km) north of Las Vegas. It's in barren, desert terrain, an area of dry lakes and low mountains, creosote bushes and Joshua trees. It is surrounded by the Nevada Test and Training Range (NTTR), a 5,000-square-mile

The sparsely populated Nevada desert lends itself to the otherworldly speculation surrounding the government facility of Area 51.

(13,000 sq km) piece of the Nevada desert as big as the state of Connecticut. It also abuts the U.S. Department of Energy's Nevada National Security Site, a 1,360-square-mile (3,500 sq km) area where nearly 1,000 nuclear weapons were tested from the 1950s through the 1990s. Area 51 itself covers about 600 square miles (1,554 sq km) and is surrounded by heavy security both on and above the ground. Even air force pilots from the training range are forbidden from flying into the airspace above Area 51; those who cut even a corner are escorted to the ground by fighter jets and intensely interrogated. On the ground, security cameras and motion detectors ring the site. Hikers encounter signs telling them that the use of deadly force is authorized to keep them out, and are often quickly met by security guards in Jeeps. No one knows exactly who employs the guards, who wear camouflage and thus are known casually as "camo dudes."

Area 51 most likely got its name from the scheme that was used to name sections of the NTTR. The range is divided into nearly 30 numbered areas, 1 through 30. But there are no areas numbered 31 through 50. Some people think Area 51 may have gotten its name because it is next to Area 15, but no one is sure. Over the years, officials and pilots have called it "Watertown," "Paradise Ranch," "The Box," and "Dreamland."

In 2013, documents revealed the U.S. used Area 51 to test aircraft, including several "secretly acquired" models from the Soviet Union.

Why put an important military operation out in the desert? In the 1930s, that part of the Nevada desert was a wild country, far from any towns or people and home to deer and wild horses. But in the 1950s, president Dwight Eisenhower ordered the development of a

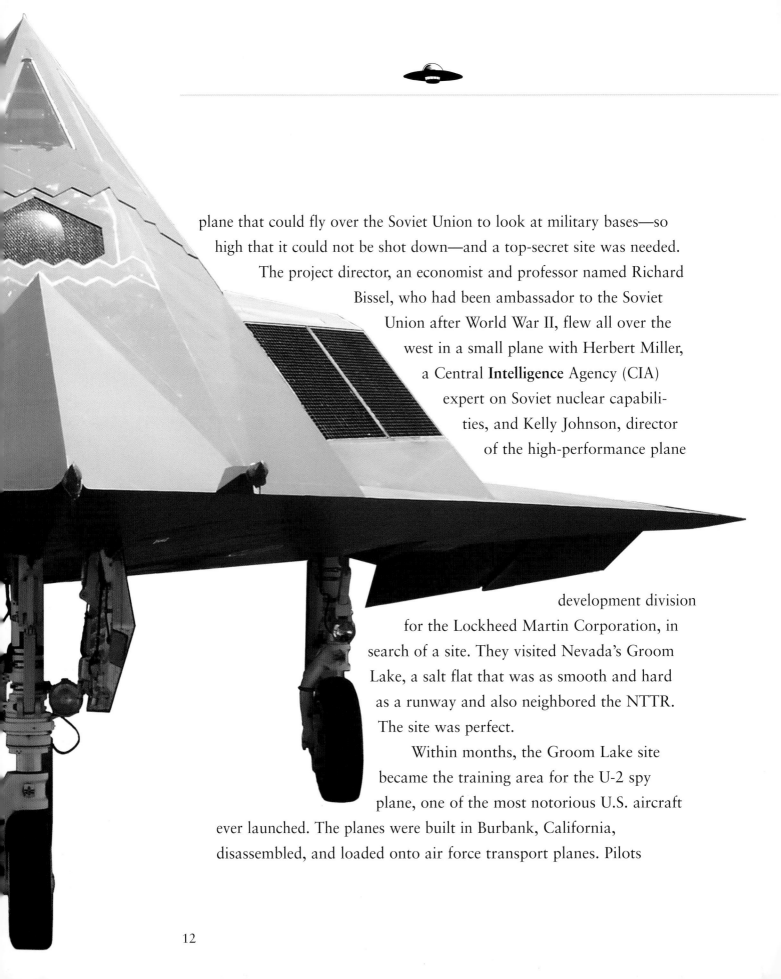

plane that could fly over the Soviet Union to look at military bases—so high that it could not be shot down—and a top-secret site was needed. The project director, an economist and professor named Richard Bissel, who had been ambassador to the Soviet Union after World War II, flew all over the west in a small plane with Herbert Miller, a Central **Intelligence** Agency (CIA) expert on Soviet nuclear capabilities, and Kelly Johnson, director of the high-performance plane

development division for the Lockheed Martin Corporation, in search of a site. They visited Nevada's Groom Lake, a salt flat that was as smooth and hard as a runway and also neighbored the NTTR. The site was perfect.

Within months, the Groom Lake site became the training area for the U-2 spy plane, one of the most notorious U.S. aircraft ever launched. The planes were built in Burbank, California, disassembled, and loaded onto air force transport planes. Pilots

carrying the parts took off not knowing what their destination was, only that they would receive instructions on the way. When they had descended to hundreds of feet above the ground, into what looked like utter darkness, the Area 51 runway lights flashed on and guided them in. Moments after they landed, the lights shut off again.

Though it quickly became a key part of U.S. defense activities, Area 51 was cleared of people in 1957 after a 74-**kiloton** nuclear bomb, the Hood bomb, was detonated in a test nearby, saturating the area with plutonium, a **radioactive** material deadly to humans. The bomb was six times more powerful than those dropped on Hiroshima and Nagasaki, Japan, in 1945. It is still the largest nuclear bomb ever to have been detonated over the continental U.S. Area 51 remained closed and deserted until January 1960, when the air force began designing a plane invisible to radar that would fly higher and faster than the U-2. The Area 51 runway was extended to nearly 6 miles (9.7 km) in length, and the restricted airspace above it was expanded from 50 square miles (129 sq km) to 440 square miles (1,140 sq km). That allowed for development of the Archangel 12, known more simply as the A-12; and later the SR-71 Blackbird, which flew in the Persian Gulf War of the early 1990s; and the F-117 Nighthawk, a dominant player in the Persian Gulf as well as in the War on Terror.

Such engineering has made Area 51 a busy place, although it is still remote and inhospitable. It is windy and dusty there, with temperatures that can fluctuate from 100 °F (37.8 °C) on summer days to 0 °F (-17.8 °C) on winter nights, with daily temperature swings of 40 degrees considered normal. Yet the air force, CIA, and Lockheed ultimately installed barracks, dining halls, and other amenities for hundreds of workers, whom they

The military's development of such aircraft as stealth fighters (opposite) and U-2s (above) remained carefully guarded secrets at Area 51.

flew to Area 51 weekly from Las Vegas on commercial jets with the windows covered. On the ground, workers were often shuttled from place to place on buses, also with windows blacked out.

It wasn't until 1978 that the city of Rachel, Nevada, was established along Route 375 about 25 miles (40 km) outside the east gate of Area 51, giving official status to the ramshackle collection of homes for about 100 people. Rachel was as close as anyone without high-level **security clearance** or a sturdy vehicle could get to Area 51, so over time it attracted a steady stream of people curious about secret aircraft, lights in the night sky, **sonic booms,** and what seemed to be a concentration of unidentified flying objects (UFOs). And after Bob Lazar's interviews in the late 1980s, the small town became internationally known.

Like Rachel, Nevada, the city of Roswell, New Mexico, became associated with odd happenings— and extraterrestrial possibilities.

A Good Guess

The U.S. Air Force designed its F-117 Nighthawk to avoid radar detection, but a plastic model turned out to be anything but invisible to consumers. A designer for Testor Corporation, John Andrews, used publicly available information—filling in gaps with his own understanding of military aircraft—to design a model of the stealth fighter he guessed the air force was building at Area 51 in the early 1980s. Testor unveiled its F-19 Stealth Fighter model in 1986, and although, or perhaps *because*, the air force refused to acknowledge the plane existed, Testor soon sold more than 700,000 of the models, making it the most popular aircraft model ever. Once the F-117 was publicly revealed two years later, people realized that the model was very different from the real thing. Still, the popularity of the model and the refusal by the air force to acknowledge anything about the real plane prompted hearings to be held in Congress, an example of how secrecy can work against itself. Andrews regarded models as teaching tools, and although he was an army veteran, he was also critical of the government for concealing information from its own citizens. He died in 1999.

A MAN-MADE MYSTERY

Area 51 has always placed a premium on secrecy. As a project developed in part by the CIA, the lead U.S. intelligence-gathering agency, the site's concealment was of top importance. The remote location in the desert aided that effort, but the secrecy went much farther. Employees and even supervisors were often not told what their work was about or how it related to work others were doing, and they were forbidden from discussing it. Even in the 1980s, after the workforce had swelled to a reported 2,000 people (which would have placed it among Nevada's 20 largest cities, had the workers lived there), employees had to sign pledges stating that they would not discuss their work or even their workplace with anybody, under penalty of 10 years in prison or a $10,000 fine.

As a result, the work at Area 51 became known as "black projects," their cost and purpose concealed even from Congress. (It's been reported that the Area 51 budget is about $1 billion per year.) When an A-12 from Area 51 crashed in Utah in 1963 and a vacationing family came upon the wreckage, CIA officials who had pursued the aircraft confiscated the film from their camera and paid them off in cash. Similarly, in 1962, when a Greyhound bus scraped against a trailer carrying parts of an A-12 to

In the late '90s, conspiracy theorists saw the evasiveness of Bill Clinton's (opposite) administration as proof of Area 51's deceptive activities.

Area 51, officials quickly and quietly authorized payment of $5,000 for damages to the bus to prevent an insurance claim or any other kind of legal process.

When some workers who had developed diseases they believed to have been caused by the burning of toxic materials at Area 51 (not even the trash was allowed to be carried out, so everything was destroyed on site), they went to court in 1994 to discover the truth. However, the government sealed all records related to the case, even those of the workers' lawyer, preventing the public from seeing them. The government even refused to admit whether there was jet fuel or paint on the site. President Bill Clinton then exempted Area 51 from Environmental Protection Agency requirements that inventories of hazardous waste be made public, and in 1998, the courts ruled that the trial could not continue, since the government would not provide key information. Area 51's special exemption has been renewed every year since then.

But the case cracked the walls of secrecy around Area 51. More than

finally acknowledged in the court proceedings that it had "an operating location near Groom Lake." But that was all.

The government may have surrounded Area 51 with secrecy to prevent other nations from learning about American military technology. But the secrecy had a peculiar effect on the U.S. itself. In 1947, shortly after the end of World War II, when international relations were tense and uncertain, there was a mysterious aircraft crash in the desert outside Roswell, New Mexico. First described even by the U.S. Army as a flying saucer—an account that was amended within a day—the occurrence was part of a wave of UFO reports that endured for several years.

According to a CIA report released in 1997, the agency had investigated nearly 1,000 UFO reports by 1951, often interviewing citizen-witnesses but swearing them to secrecy. Faced with a public that seemed convinced that UFOs had come from elsewhere in the universe, guided by intelligent beings using sophisticated technology, the government was in a delicate spot. If aliens really had landed, apparently without warning, could the government tell the public that they had? Wouldn't people begin to doubt the government's defense systems? If any extraterrestrials had survived, where were they? Were they in our midst, somehow? One idea that emerged was that extraterrestrials had come to capture human organs, because their own were failing. According to the theory, the government and the visitors had struck a deal: the visitors could capture humans and extract certain organs, while the government would learn from the extraterrestrials how to build aircraft like theirs—extremely fast, capable of

Interest in the Roswell incident was renewed in 1980 with a book featuring "eyewitness accounts" of the wreckage and cover-up.

hovering and darting from side to side, and able to accelerate with unimaginable quickness. So if the government was engaged in developing sophisticated aircraft at Area 51, it stood to reason (to some) that aliens were also being held there. And that seemed to explain the secrecy.

The U.S. citizenry had been carried away by UFO dramas in the past—most notably in 1938, when a dramatic radio broadcast based on the novel *War of the Worlds* caused a national panic and led people to believe Earth had been invaded by aliens who had landed in New Jersey. Reaction to the broadcast, which was designed to mimic a series of news bulletins, was intense enough that phone lines in some cities were overloaded with

callers checking with neighbors. For a time in the early 1960s, the CIA was concerned that a similar hoax could divert the nation's air defense system so thoroughly that the U.S. would be vulnerable to an air assault from a real enemy, such as the Soviet Union. For a while, the air force cooperated with ufologists, but author Annie Jacobsen, in her book *Area 51: An Uncensored History of America's Top Secret Military Base*, asserts that such teamwork simply allowed the CIA to investigate the people who had collected vast amounts of information about UFOs and find out what they knew.

Though Orson Welles's radio broadcast caused confusion, many researchers now suggest the media exaggerated the extent of the panic.

A series of governmental commissions through the 1950s and '60s determined that UFOs were not real, and some accounts assert that this caused the press to lose interest in the subject. Against this backdrop, Area 51's secret expansion continued well into the 1980s. Some historians argue that there were two reasons why the government was willing to allow UFOs to be the subject of public controversy: The first was that the attention encouraged support for anything that looked like the government's investigation into the mystery, even though governmental commissions tended to dismiss the notion of UFOs. The second was that speculation about UFOs diverted attention from the development and testing of very real aeronautical breakthroughs at Area 51, such as the U-2 and other spy and fighter planes.

Despite scientific attempts to debunk UFOs, sightings continued. In 1975, radar over the U.S. and Canada tracked the most UFOs ever in a single wave, but the North American Aerospace Defense Command (the same institution that every December tracks the whereabouts of another mysterious figure: Santa Claus) said helicopters failed to confirm a single one. In the 1980s, sightings of black triangles over Belgium caused a stir. And through the years, some scholars have suggested that uncertainties about UFOs might be more important than official sources acknowledge. In 1966, a group of scientists determined that 15 percent of UFO sightings could not be explained as planes, weather balloons, gas, or other common occurrences—a far higher share than the 9 percent a government inquiry found. As far back as 1960, the Brookings Institution declared that, while the discovery of intelligent life elsewhere in the universe was "not likely," it also "could happen at any time." So what were those hovering, darting, intensely bright lights people kept seeing above Area 51?

Some believe flying triangles are untraceable by satellite, while skeptics explain the shapes as results of electrical plasma or other aircraft.

The Cold War At the end of World War II, the former Allied powers—the United States, Great Britain and the Soviet Union—disagreed on how to rebuild Europe. The Soviet Union wanted to control its neighbors and spread communism. The U.S. and Great Britain wanted to establish capitalist, democratic states in places that had been destroyed during the war. All had seen the destructive power of the world's first atomic bomb, dropped by the U.S. over Japan in 1945, and understood the dangerous potential of that technology. But the nations were also at odds. So they resorted to a new way of fighting: the Cold War. It was a conflict in which, for nearly 50 years, the U.S. and Soviet Union spent billions building and testing weapons but not using them against one another, for fear of triggering nuclear retaliation. Political tensions forced many nations to choose sides, and fueled actual wars in places such as Korea and Vietnam. And, of course, the Cold War made spying into an international industry, supported by secrecy. That led directly to the development of Area 51 as a test site for breakthrough aircraft. Without Cold War espionage, Area 51 may never have existed, even in fiction.

FOLKS
AND
FICTION

Legends surround Bob Lazar. Most of them were of his own making, outlined in several television interviews in Las Vegas in 1989, in which he tore off the cloak of secrecy regarding UFO landings and aliens that had surrounded Area 51 for nearly 40 years. In the early 1980s, Lazar was operating a business out of his Las Vegas home, processing photographic film for real estate appraisers. The business was successful, but what was more notable was that Lazar delivered his processed film in a jet-powered car he had designed himself.

Hydrogen bombs have never been used in warfare, but during tests, Teller's "H-bomb" had 700 times the power of the atomic bomb.

About that time, Lazar, who claimed to have earned master's degrees in both electronic technology from the California Institute of Technology and physics from the Massachusetts Institute of Technology, was attending a conference where he spotted Edward Teller, known as the "Father of the Hydrogen Bomb." Teller was reading a newspaper article about Lazar and his car. Lazar introduced himself, and later Teller invited him to come to

work on a project in Nevada involving aircraft.

Lazar signed an oath swearing he'd never reveal what he was working on and agreed to have his phone tapped and his car and home searched without warning. He reported to the Las Vegas airport, was flown to a base north of the city, and was taken in a bus with blacked-out windows to a facility where he saw a large, disk-shaped craft with tiny seats in a hangar. He was taken to a room, handed a large stack of material to study, and left alone. When his escort closed the door, Lazar spotted a poster on the back of the door that showed a picture of a dry lakebed with a saucer-like craft and the words "They're here."

Over time, Lazar determined the vehicles in the hangar—he saw or read reports about nine of them—had been fueled by **Element** 115, a substance Lazar theorized could have unique gravitational properties as it decayed, allowing aircraft to travel great distances. He also claimed to have read **autopsy** reports of bodies that had been in the aircraft, referring to them as "The Kids" and describing them as short and hairless, with large heads and almond-shaped eyes. He even glimpsed a living one through the window of a room as he was being ushered past. He studied documents stating that the spacecraft had come from Zeta Reticuli, a **binary** star system 200 trillion miles (322 trillion km) away. Several years before, a husband and wife who claimed they'd been abducted by aliens had said their abductors had come from Zeta Reticuli.

Lazar had come to believe that what had already been learned at Area 51 needed the involvement of more scientists, not secrecy. "Just the concept

Researchers have recreated the strangely shaped, human-like bodies several witnesses described from incidents such as Roswell.

29

Tourists—believers and skeptics alike—visit southern Nevada because of its notorious reputation for alien and UFO sightings.

that there's definite proof, and we can even have articles from another world, another system . . . you can't just not tell everyone," Lazar said.

But when Lazar was caught with several friends trying to get a closer look at what he'd told them were test flights of disks at Area 51, he was fired. A short time later he gave his interview on Las Vegas television in a way that concealed his identity. But after he was run off the highway and shot at in his car by people he believed were trying to guard Area 51's secrecy, he decided to reveal himself on television, as a way of protecting himself. He quickly became a folk hero to ufologists and for a while was co-host of a Las Vegas radio show. However, his story was undermined when the universities he claimed to have attended reported they had no records of him. Lazar said the government had stolen the evidence and even destroyed his birth certificate, but the damage was done.

Like Lazar, Glenn Campbell called himself a "lobbyist for openness." Campbell, who had made some money designing a computer program for banks, moved from Boston to Rachel, Nevada, in 1993 after the air force expanded the restricted area surrounding Area 51. Working in a bar-restaurant in the desert outpost and calling himself "Psychospy," Campbell set up the organizations called Secrecy Oversight Council and Whitesides Defense Committee (named for nearby Whitesides Mountain, which for years had offered an overlook of Area 51 before the air force declared it off-limits). He published his own document (*The Area 51 Viewers' Guide*), advised the growing number of visitors on their rights and the proper responses if confronted by security agents when venturing close to Area 51, and posted a regular online newsletter called "The Groom Lake Desert Rat," a wide-ranging compendium of news, science, speculation, policy, and

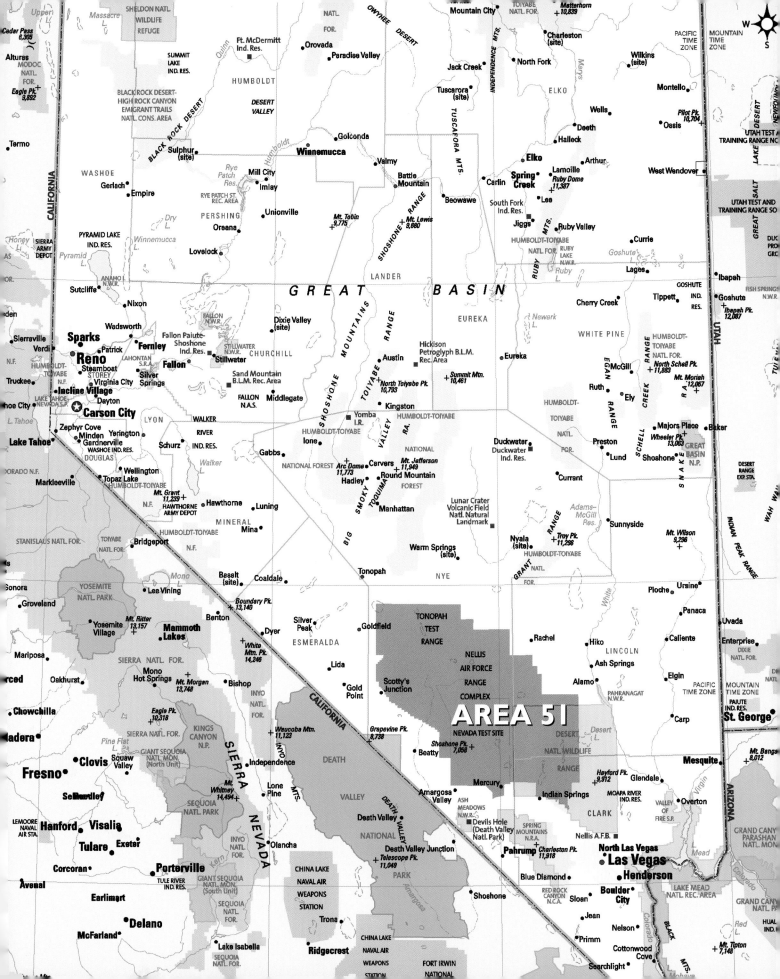

politics. Campbell called the trailer he moved into the "Area 51 Research Center." He explored and marked a route to an overlook just outside Area 51 that he named "Freedom Ridge." In 1994, he took a Nevada state legislator up Freedom Ridge to show him how the activity and development at Area 51 proved the air force hadn't been paying enough property taxes to surrounding Lincoln County. Campbell also published the radio frequencies that the Area 51 security guards used, as well as arrival and departure times for the planes carrying workers from and to Las Vegas.

Campbell was in some ways the opposite of Lazar and the people who came to Rachel to get close to Area 51 and perhaps connect with aliens. He didn't believe in aliens. His *Viewers' Guide* warns people that the most dangerous creatures they might encounter are not aliens or security patrols but cows. In an interview with author David Darlington for his book *Area 51: The Dreamland Chronicles*, Campbell said the community of UFO followers "is full of nuts and ridiculous folklore" and that UFO sightings simply are examples of people's imaginations at work. "When people look at a light in the sky, what they see indicates something about what's inside of them," he said. "I'm not into UFOs," he said. "I'm into humanity and philosophy."

Lazar and Campbell were part of an eccentric band of Area 51 monitors that occasionally put the town of Rachel in the national news. But they couldn't have done it without the UFOs and extraterrestrials.

Underlying Area 51's mysteriousness is the notion that it is the place where the remains of the 1947 Roswell crash are being kept, examined, and perhaps duplicated. That possibility has sparked the imaginations not only of ufologists but also of the Nevada tourism industry, Hollywood, and other generators of American popular culture.

People such as Glenn Campbell sought to demystify, or explain, the restricted location of Area 51 and its secret government activities.

One of the grandest conspiracy theories of all time claims the U.S. faked the 1969 moon landing through camera trickery.

The Indiana Jones movie *The Kingdom of the Crystal Skull* expanded the mystery even further by suggesting that the remains of the Ark of the Covenant were stored at Area 51. Several elements of Lazar's story—such as Zeta Reticuli and Element 115—were key features of the television series *Seven Days*, which dealt with a time-traveling spacecraft developed from the Roswell remains. The 1996 action film *Independence Day* used Area 51 as the place where the president was taken to hide from attacking aliens and where the Roswell remains were used to repel the attack and ultimately save the world from annihilation. A 2005 video game, *Area 51*, is built on the notion of aliens trading their technological know-how for human test subjects who would provide them with a virus to use in a war in their home world. And some who argue that the 1969 Apollo moon landing was a hoax say it was all filmed at Area 51.

The television series *The X-Files* located one of its episodes in Rachel, Nevada, the tiny unincorporated city outside of Area 51. In real life, Rachel has styled itself as "The UFO Capital of the World." In 2006, the town received publicity when KFC installed an 87,500-square-foot (8,130 sq m) tile version of its logo on the desert floor on the edge of Rachel, announcing that it would be the only business logo visible from space. (The company removed it in 2007.) Meanwhile, Rachel has become a draw for **geocachers**, thanks to the 1,500 geocaches placed along Route 375, the "Extraterrestrial Highway," in 2011.

Saucers: Keep Left Nevada Route 375 carries the usual traffic—cars, trucks, and motorcycles—through nearly 100 miles (161 km) of desert from Ash Springs to Warm Springs. But could some of those headlights belong to a vehicle of unknown origin? Possibly, since the road has been officially designated as the Extraterrestrial Highway. The road runs within about 25 miles (40.2 km) of Area 51, closer than any other major thoroughfare to the site long rumored to be a place where researchers were working with captured UFOs and aliens. The designation accompanied the promotion of the 1996 20th Century Fox film *Independence Day*, in which Area 51 is a key location. When the Nevada legislature nixed the highway name change, governor Bob Miller got the state transportation board to authorize it anyway.

The 1996 dedication at the Little A-Le-Inn in Rachel, Nevada, was attended by numerous movie stars and a person claiming to represent the "intergalactic tourism association." The highway, still one of the least-traveled roads in Nevada, is now posted with green signs showing pictures of flying saucers. But even though it passes through wide-open, lonely country, drivers still have to watch how fast they're going. The speed limit is Warp 7.

STRAIGHT STORIES, STRANGER STORIES

Some of the cloud of mystery around Area 51 has evaporated in recent years. Details of the U-2 project were **declassified** in 1998, allowing it to be known—more than 40 years after the fact—that pilot Ray Goudey had been the first man to fly a plane higher than 65,000 feet (19,812 m).

In 2007, decades after workers at Area 51 would hustle the A-12 into a hangar several times a day to keep it from being viewed by satellites, the CIA displayed an A-12 in front of its Langley, Virginia, headquarters, as part of the agency's 60th anniversary celebration. The public was allowed to stroll by a titanium-skinned aircraft that could fly up to an altitude of 90,000 feet (27,432 m) at 3 times the speed of sound. It was still the only plane capable of flying that high and that fast. Before the 1964 presidential election, President Johnson, eager to illustrate American progress on defense technology, wanted to make the A-12 public. An aide told him it was for "strategic **reconnaissance**." Johnson, apparently latching on to the first letter of each of those words, made a public revelation about a new spy plane called the SR-71. The SR-71 Blackbird thus got all the press attention, while the CIA's A-12 was able to remain a secret. The A-12 has rarely been seen in flight, although it is believed that many reported UFO sightings have been extremely fast and highly reflective A-12s.

In the early days of stealth technology, the Blackbird was groundbreaking. Such aircraft used angled surfaces and materials in their design that absorbed radar beams rather than reflecting them back to radar antennae and allowing the planes to be tracked. On radar, the 107-foot-long (32.6 m) Blackbird, with a wingspan of nearly 58 feet (17.7 m), appeared to have an area of 108 square feet (10 sq m). Thirty-two SR-71s were built, and most had long careers: the air force flew them from 1964 to 1998. But designers

In 1964, President Johnson (above) unveiled the SR-71 (opposite), designed by Lockheed's so-called "Skunk Works" division.

and air force officials felt the plane, or at least its radar image, was still too big. The air force's F-117 Nighthawk (active from 1981 to 2008) represented a vast improvement in radar-evasion technology. Although it was 66 feet (20.1 m) long with a wingspan of 43 feet (13.1 m), the bat-shaped aircraft appeared on radar to be the same size as a ball bearing! Area 51 might have needed secrecy to operate in its first three decades, but now it was producing secrecy itself, in a way.

For many years, aviation buffs and ufologists had asserted that a plane called the Aurora, capable of flying at five times the speed of sound, was under development at Area 51. That is still largely regarded as legend. But in the meantime, Area 51 saw the development of an even newer concept in aircraft: unmanned flights.

Drone technology—flying aircraft by remote control—was first used in World War II, though it did not meet with great success then. In fact,

With wingspans of 48.7 feet (14.8 m), unmanned Predator drones provide reconnaissance, combat, and air support.

the older brother of President Kennedy was killed over Germany in 1944 when a bomber from which he was supposed to eject (allowing it to be guided to its target by another plane nearby) exploded. But the CIA pursued the idea, producing the Predator drone in the 1990s for reconnaissance purposes.

By 2000, concerned about the activities of al Qaeda terrorist Osama bin Laden, the CIA outfitted the Predator with Hellfire missiles, and, for training, built a mockup of bin Laden's compound in Afghanistan on the edge of Area 51. Drone reconnaissance and missiles enabled the CIA to kill al Qaeda operative Qaed Salim Sinan al-Harethi in the desert of Yemen in 2002. In 2012, according to reports, Predators flying in the Middle East were being operated by "pilots" at computers just outside Area 51.

In August 2013, the government officially acknowledged the existence of Area 51 by declassifying a 1992 CIA report. Some believed the move indicated the government was becoming less secretive, while others

During the decade-long manhunt for Osama bin Laden, drones helped locate and monitor the elusive terrorist leader.

wondered if the news was meant to prepare the public for the truth about alien activities. In nearby Rachel, declassifications have enabled former A-12 workers to meet in reunions, some at the Little A-le-Inn. Even former CIA staffers show up. The group has called itself Roadrunners Internationale. Its purpose is to preserve the history of Area 51 and the people who worked there on some of history's most influential aircraft. The group's website provides details on equipment, training, and who flew what planes how often, as well as photographs and a list of where the remaining A-12s can now be seen. The reunions are often covered by news media but also have the flavor of a meeting of any business or alumni association. Members swap stories, play golf, and sell memorabilia—including the only official CIA material allowed for sale outside CIA headquarters at Langley.

Declassification has also provided dramatic twists to the tales that have long surrounded Area 51. In her 2011 book, Annie Jacobsen reports that the disks that crashed at Roswell in 1947 were most definitely not from another planet. They were from the Soviet Union—a fact that could be determined from the **Cyrillic** writing inside the craft. The Soviets apparently had exploited disk-flight technology developed by German Nazis whom they had either captured or were still in contact with after World War II. But then the book makes an even more dramatic assertion. Quoting an unnamed engineer who worked on the remains of the crash, Jacobsen writes that the creatures in the craft were human children, whose large heads and strange eyes were in fact examples of human experimentation performed by Nazis during and after World War II, under an agreement between the Nazis and Soviet dictator Joseph Stalin. Stalin, the engineer was told, believed that by sending the small aviators in a disk to crash in the U.S., he could cause a panic in

Cyrillic characters found in the Roswell craft would be consistent with witnesses' reports of seeing strange inscriptions among the wreckage.

the U.S. that the government might be unable to handle. Area 51 workers who were extensively quoted elsewhere in the book said after it was published that they were unaware of any such things happening at Area 51 and were shocked to read about them.

These days, the town of Rachel is quieter than it used to be. After the air force expanded the secure zone around Area 51 in 1995 to include Freedom Ridge, Glenn Campbell, founder of the Area 51 Research Center, left. The center closed several years later. In 2013, the only operating business in Rachel was the Little A-le-Inn ("Earthlings Welcome!"), home of the "Alien Burger." On the restaurant's website, owner Pat Travis sums up why she's still there: "Life is a mystery. Enjoy the ride." Indeed, no matter how many documents get declassified or how many reports of UFOs are debunked, Area 51, or some other place like it, will continue to draw people seeking contact with other worlds and eager to probe the mysteries that surround them.

Communist leader Joseph Stalin murdered and imprisoned millions in his quest to turn the Soviet Union into a world power.

Roswell Accounts of flying objects carrying strange visitors go back thousands of years. But the modern UFO era can be traced to 1946, perhaps because World War II, which had featured extensive combat in the air, brought new awareness of the dangers the skies could bring. In 1946 alone, there was a six-week wave of UFO sightings in the Pacific Northwest. But the next year, a crash near Roswell, New Mexico, was a game-changer. An army information officer put out a news release saying a saucer had crashed, and the news went international. The next day, the army took back its statement and claimed the object had been a weather balloon. In the 1990s, the air force said the debris had come from a device designed to detect Soviet nuclear tests, but by then "Roswell" had become synonymous with tales of alien visitors to Earth and associated government cover-ups. Roswell's reputation also involved Area 51, situated nearly 1,000 miles (1,609 km) west. According to the story, whatever crashed near Roswell, including live alien crew members, was taken to Wright-Patterson Air Force base in Ohio—some say by tunnel, though it's 2,000 miles (3,219 km) away—and then removed to Area 51 for further research.

Field Notes

aeronautics: the study or practice of aircraft navigation

autopsy: an examination of a dead body to determine the cause of death.

binary: having two parts

budget: the amount of money required to operate a household, office, government, or other enterprise. Government budgets are usually renewed yearly or every other year

conspiracies: secret plans, involving several or many participants, to accomplish something unlawful or harmful

Cyrillic: an alphabet derived from the Greek alphabet and used for Slavic languages, including Russian

declassified: opened to the public; no longer secret

element: a substance that cannot be broken down into simpler components

geocachers: people who, for recreation, find items hidden in the landscape by using global positioning devices

intelligence: information having military, political, or other strategic value

irony: the occurrence of the opposite of what might be expected

kiloton: an explosive force equivalent to 1,000 metric tons of TNT

radioactive: emitting ionizing radiation or particles

reconnaissance: a search for useful military information

security clearance: permission to enter guarded places or read certain secret material

sonic booms: explosive sounds made by the compression of sound waves as an object moves at the speed of sound

Selected Bibliography

Campbell, Glenn. *Area 51 Viewer's Guide.* Rachel, Nev.: Area 51 Research Center, 1995.

Darlington, David. *Area 51: The Dreamland Chronicles; The Legend of America's Most Secret Military Base.* New York: Henry Holt, 1997.

Hansen, Terry. *The Psychology of Dreamland: How Secrecy is Destroying Public Faith in Government and Science.* http://www.abovetopsecret .com/forum/thread60181/pg1.

Jacobsen, Annie. *Area 51: An Uncensored History of America's Top Secret Military Base.* New York: Little, Brown, 2011.

Patton, Phil. *Dreamland: Travels Inside the Secret World of Roswell and Area 51.* New York: Villard, 1998.

Rich, Ben, and Leo Janos. *Skunk Works: A Personal Memoir of My Years at Lockheed.* New York: Little, Brown, 1994.

Wright, Susan. *UFO Headquarters: Investigations on Current Exraterrestrial Activity.* New York: St. Martin's Press, 1998.

Websites

SECRET HEROES

http://area51specialprojects.com/

History, photos, biographies, and personal accounts of Area 51 by people who served there.

UFOMIND

http://www.ufomind.com/area51/

Area 51 history, geography, corporate and military connections, photos, news articles, and back issues of "The Desert Rat" newsletter.

Note: *Every effort has been made to ensure that the websites listed above are suitable for children, that they have educational value, and that they contain no inappropriate material. However, because of the nature of the Internet, it is impossible to guarantee that these sites will remain active indefinitely or that their contents will not be altered.*

Index

A

aircraft 9, 12, 13, 14, 15, 18,
    19, 20, 23, 24, 25, 29, 38,
    40–41, 43
  Archangel 12 (A-12) 13, 18,
    38, 41, 43
  drones 40, 41
  F-117 Nighthawk 13, 15, 40
  SR-71 Blackbird 13, 38
  U-2 12, 13, 19, 24, 38
Andrews, John 15
Area 51 Research Center 33, 44

B

Bissel, Richard 12
budgets 8, 18
Burbank, California 12

C

Campbell, Glenn 30, 33, 44
Cold War 12, 25
  and espionage 12, 25

E

employees 4, 8, 13–14, 18, 19,
    33, 38, 43, 44
  and Roadrunners
    Internationale 43
extraterrestrial life 5, 9, 20, 23,
    24, 28, 29, 33, 35, 43, 45
  and reports of abductions
    20, 29

J

Jacobsen, Annie 23, 43
Johnson, Kelly 12
Johnson, Lyndon B. 8, 38

L

Langley, Virginia 38, 43
Lazar, Bob 4, 5, 14, 28–30, 33
Lockheed Martin Corporation
    12, 13

M

media portrayals 34, 35
Miller, Herbert 12

N

name 10
Nevada 4, 9, 10, 12, 14, 18,
    20, 28, 29, 30, 33, 34, 35,
    43, 44
  Extraterrestrial Highway 14,
    34, 35
  Freedom Ridge 33, 44
  Groom Lake 12, 20
  Las Vegas 4, 9, 14, 28, 29,
    30, 33
  National Security Site 10
  Rachel 14, 30, 33, 34, 35,
    43, 44
  Test and Training Range
    (NTTR) 9, 10, 12
North American Aerospace
    Defense Command 24
nuclear weapons 10, 12, 13,
    25, 45

R

Roswell, New Mexico 20, 33,
    43, 45

S

secrecy 5, 8, 12, 15, 18, 19,
    20, 23, 28, 29, 30, 38, 40,
    41, 43, 44
  and declassification 15, 38,
    41, 43, 44
  exemptions 19
  sealed records 19
security 10, 30, 33
Soviet Union 12, 23, 25, 43, 45

T

Teller, Edward 28
tourism 33, 35

U

UFOs 14, 20, 23–24, 28, 33,
    34, 35, 38, 44, 45
  and radio programs 23
  reported sightings 20, 24,
    33, 38, 44, 45
U.S. Air Force 10, 12, 13, 15,
    23, 30, 33, 38, 40, 44, 45
  Wright-Patterson Air Force
    Base 45
U.S. government 4–5, 8, 9, 12,
    13, 18, 19–20, 23, 24, 30,
    34, 38, 41, 43, 44, 45
  Central Intelligence Agency
    (CIA) 12, 13, 18, 20,
    23, 38, 41, 43
  conspiracy theories 4, 9, 20,
    23, 30, 34, 45
  counterterrorism 41
  defense 8, 13, 20, 23, 38